No One Loves
Us Here

Ross Howard

A SAMUEL FRENCH ACTING EDITION

SAMUEL
FRENCH
FOUNDED 1830

SAMUELFRENCH.COM
SAMUELFRENCH-LONDON.CO.UK

FOR PRODUCTION ENQUIRIES

UNITED STATES AND CANADA
Info@Samuelfrench.com
1-866-598-8449

UNITED KINGDOM AND EUROPE
Plays@SamuelFrench-London.co.uk
020-7255-4302

Each title is subject to availability from Samuel French, depending upon country of performance. Please be aware that *NO ONE LOVES US HERE* may not be licensed by Samuel French in your territory. Professional and amateur producers should contact the nearest Samuel French office or licensing partner to verify availability.

MUSIC USE NOTE

Licensees are solely responsible for obtaining formal written permission from copyright owners to use copyrighted music in the performance of this play and are strongly cautioned to do so. If no such permission is obtained by the licensee, then the licensee must use only original music that the licensee owns and controls. Licensees are solely responsible and liable for all music clearances and shall indemnify the copyright owners of the play(s) and their licensing agent, Samuel French, against any costs, expenses, losses and liabilities arising from the use of music by licensees. Please contact the appropriate music licensing authority in your territory for the rights to any incidental music.

IMPORTANT BILLING AND CREDIT REQUIREMENTS

If you have obtained performance rights to this title, please refer to your licensing agreement for important billing and credit requirements.

NO ONE LOVES US HERE received a staged reading at Theatre 503, London, on 28th March 2013. The play was directed by Lydia Parker and the cast was as follows:

WASHINGTON	Nathan Clarke
MR BEAUMONT	John Schwab
MRS BEAUMONT	Christy Meyer
JACK	John Chancer
AMBER	Melli Bond

NO ONE LOVES US HERE was first produced by New Light Theater Project at Urban Stages, New York City on January 15th 2015. Directed by Jerry Heymann. The cast was as follows:

WASHINGTON	Anthony Michael Irizzary
MR BEAUMONT	Christian Ryan
MRS BEAUMONT	Jessica Kitchens
AMBER	April Kidwell
JACK	Dick Hughes

Set Design – Brian Dudkiewicz
Costume Design – Samantha Lind
Lighting Design – Michael O'Connor
Sound Design Production – Kyle C. Norris
Stage Manager – Andrew Morton
Assistant Stage Management - Anna Clare Kerr and Abby Wylan
Technical Director – Douglas Mills
Fight Director – Scott Barrow
Producers – Michael Aguirre and Sarah Norris

POST-PRODUCTION NOTE

The playwright recommends that Scene One flows straight into Scene Two, with no transition or time lapse, and similarly between Scene Three and Scene Four.

CHARACTERS

WASHINGTON – 19, of Native American descent
MR BEAUMONT – 37
MRS BEAUMONT – 32
JACK – her father, 57
AMBER – 32

SCENE

A living room in a house in the Central Valley, California.

TIME

The present.

PRODUCTION NOTE

A dash (—) after a word denotes an interruption or an inability to complete the word or sentence. An ellipsis (…) denotes a trailing off.

ACKNOWLEDGEMENTS

Quinn M. Corbin, Jakob Holder, Harry Burton, Becca Kahane, Steve Harper, Jack Ryder, Aaron Tavaler, Kenneth Jay, Violet Patton-Ryder, Antonia Reid, William Hope and Sabrina Parker.

For Edward Emanuel

"No one loves us here."

The General in His Labyrinth, Gabriel García Marquez

No One Loves Us Here

CHARACTERS

PLACE

A living room in a house in the Central Valley, California.

TIME

The present.

A dash (-) after a word denotes an interruption or an inability to complete the word or sentence. An ellipsis (...) denotes a trailing off.

"No one loves us here."

The General in His Labyrinth, Gabriel García Marquez

Scene One

(A Sunday afternoon. Knocking on the front door. **MR.
BEAUMONT** *enters from a door leading to the rest of the
house, he has a phone to his ear but turns it off as he
opens the front door.)*

MR. BEAUMONT. Yeah?

WASHINGTON. Mr. Beaumont.

MR. BEAUMONT. Yes.

WASHINGTON. Sir, I'm from *Popcorn Video.* Your movies are
due back.

MR. BEAUMONT. Oh…are they?

WASHINGTON. I just wanted to drop by and get them.
I don't want you to have to pay a fine or anything.

MR. BEAUMONT. Oh…sure. Thanks… I guess. Come on in.

*(***WASHINGTON** *enters.)*

WASHINGTON. Thank you.

MR. BEAUMONT. How long were you knocking? We have a
doorbell.

WASHINGTON. I really prefer to knock.

MR. BEAUMONT. *(Amused)* Okay.

WASHINGTON. Your wife said I could just walk right in but
I thought that was excessive.

MR. BEAUMONT. She's still out there?

WASHINGTON. Pruning? Yes, Sir.

MR. BEAUMONT. She's obsessed with that. *(Chuckles)* They're
something aren't they? *(Stops chuckling)* Do you do this
for everyone?

WASHINGTON. What's that?

MR. BEAUMONT. Pay them a visit. Sparing them "*The Fine*".

WASHINGTON. Your wife seems nice.

MR. BEAUMONT. *(Chuckles)* Oh, Jesus.

WASHINGTON. What?

MR. BEAUMONT. There isn't an hour that goes by where I haven't considered getting myself a shotgun, waiting till she's asleep and then just unloading in her face.

WASHINGTON. You're joking.

MR. BEAUMONT. Yeah. Well, in a way. Here *(Hands him the DVDs.)* If it wasn't for all the nonsense that would come after. All the questions, the arrest, that kind of crap.

WASHINGTON. Well, you'd be smart about it.

MR. BEAUMONT. What do you mean?

WASHINGTON. I mean, you wouldn't just do it and sit there, would you?

MR. BEAUMONT. What would I do?

WASHINGTON. You'd find a way of making sure it wasn't pinned on you. You could pretend it was an intruder. Or you could just hide the body. As if she just vanished.

MR. BEAUMONT. Vanished?

WASHINGTON. Vanished. You know? Just disappeared. Like she left you or something.

MR. BEAUMONT. I don't want anyone thinking that she left me. I'm a member of the Golf club.

WASHINGTON. Cut her up in pieces and just hide each part in different places across the state. Lakes, rivers, quarries. Take a road trip. Make a couple of days of it. A labor day weekend maybe. I don't know what your work schedule is like.

MR. BEAUMONT. I make my own hours.

WASHINGTON. What are you in?

MR. BEAUMONT. Communication.

WASHINGTON. *(Looks around the living room)* You've done well.

MR. BEAUMONT. Thank you for noticing.

(Pause)

MR. BEAUMONT. Have you done this kind of thing before?

WASHINGTON. We're just talking. I work in a video store.

(Silence)

MR. BEAUMONT. Sit down. Please *(A beat)* Do you need to be anywhere?

WASHINGTON. I guess not.

MR. BEAUMONT. *(Gestures to a chair)* Then, please.

*(**WASHINGTON** sits in armchair. **MR. BEAUMONT** takes the sofa.)*

MR. BEAUMONT. You didn't tell me your name.

WASHINGTON. Can I smoke?

MR. BEAUMONT. Are you joking? In a house like this? *(Condescendingly)* Not in here, buddy.

*(**WASHINGTON** gets up to leave. **MR. BEAUMONT** gets up quickly and blocks his path to the door.)*

Just where do you think you're going?

(No response)

MR. BEAUMONT. Okay, you can smoke. Sorry. Please. Sit.

*(**WASHINGTON** sits back down on the armchair. **MR. BEAUMONT** takes the sofa once more. Silence.)*

WASHINGTON. So?

MR. BEAUMONT. Yes?

WASHINGTON. You got any cigarettes?

MR. BEAUMONT. You don't have any?

WASHINGTON. You don't have any lying around?

MR. BEAUMONT. *(Incredulously) No we don't have any lying aroun*-actually... *(remembers)* yes, yes we do. In the garage. Wait there.

*(**MR. BEAUMONT** gets up from the sofa. He walks over to the door leading to the rest of the house. He turns back briefly.)*

Don't go anywhere.

(MR. BEAUMONT exits. Moments later the front door opens and MRS. BEAUMONT appears in the doorway. She is wearing gardening gloves and is holding a large pair of pruning shears. She looks around the room and sees WASHINGTON alone.)

MRS. BEAUMONT. Is he being difficult, honey? I can get the movies for you if you like.

WASHINGTON. No. Everything's fine, Mrs. Beaumont.

MRS. BEAUMONT. Are you sure?

WASHINGTON. Yes.

MRS. BEAUMONT. He's a *real* cunt.

WASHINGTON. We're fine.

MRS. BEAUMONT. *(Unsure yet cheerily)* O-kay.

(MRS. BEAUMONT exits and closes the front door behind her as she continues in the front garden. A couple of seconds later MR. BEAUMONT enters with an open pack of cigarettes.)

MR. BEAUMONT. I knew we still got 'em. Some asshole left them here on New Year's Eve.

(He hands them to WASHINGTON.)

WASHINGTON. Light?

MR. BEAUMONT. I knew you'd ask that.

(MR. BEAUMONT takes a box of matches from his pocket and hands them to WASHINGTON. MR. BEAUMONT sits back down on the sofa. WASHINGTON lights a cigarette and begins to smoke.)

Those things'll kill you, you know.

(WASHINGTON looks over next to him for something to tap his ash into. He picks up an urn, opens it.)

Not in there. That's my mom. Take that little plate.

(WASHINGTON puts the lid back on the urn and places it back on the table. He picks up the little plate and rests it on his lap.)

MR. BEAUMONT. So what's your name?

WASHINGTON. Washington.

MR. BEAUMONT. Are you serious?

WASHINGTON. Deadly.

MR. BEAUMONT. No kidding.

WASHINGTON. *(Points to his face)* Redskins.

MR. BEAUMONT. Wow, your folks must be something else, right? Real characters. So what do they do?

WASHINGTON. Give their child up.

(Brief silence)

MR. BEAUMONT. I'm sorry.

WASHINGTON. It was a long time ago. I'm over it.

MR. BEAUMONT. Jeez. I could never do that. Hand over my kid *(Points towards the front door)* She can't have any. Fucking useless.

WASHINGTON. *(Without any great feeling)* Must be tough.

MR. BEAUMONT. Always liked the idea of that. An offspring. I'm not talking about babies so much, they always seemed kinda boring to me. Sure, they're cute but so are dogs, you know what I mean? *(A beat)* Now that's an animal. Stupid, but loyal. You can't put a price on that.

WASHINGTON. No.

MR. BEAUMONT. And then babies turn to kids, and that's never really grabbed me either. Driving them here, driving them there, spilling all kinds of crap on the back seat. *(Laughs)* I guess it's all paying your dues, huh? Like building a business from nothing. When they become men, that's where the true satisfaction is, I bet. Following in your footsteps. Like father, like son. Go fishing. Something with your stamp on, you know? Your mark. *(A beat)*

Maybe someday. Great thing about being a man, right? You got time. *(A beat)* Do you live locally?

WASHINGTON. It depends.

MR. BEAUMONT. On what?

WASHINGTON. I'm couch surfing for the moment. So sometimes I'm local, sometimes I'm not.

MR. BEAUMONT. Why's that?

WASHINGTON. I just had to get out. You know.

MR. BEAUMONT. Right. Hey stuff happens.

WASHINGTON. Yes.

MR. BEAUMONT. So how long have you worked at *Blockbuster*?

WASHINGTON. *Popcorn-*

MR. BEAUMONT. Sorry. She goes, not me.

WASHINGTON. I've noticed *(A beat)* Four years now. Full time for the last two.

MR. BEAUMONT. Wow, that's great.

WASHINGTON. You think it's a shit job, don't you?

MR. BEAUMONT. Kinda. Does it pay?

WASHINGTON. I make more than they pay me. Not *every* movie that goes out I enter in the computer. I remember the face, remember the movie they took and I keep the money myself.

MR. BEAUMONT. Initiative.

WASHINGTON. As long as I'm in there when they bring it back and I can put it back on the shelf, everything's fine. If you pick the right times and the reliable customer, it can work out very nicely.

MR. BEAUMONT. *(Smiling)* But you reveal your secrets. I could get you fired.

WASHINGTON. You just told me that you fantasize about shooting your wife in the face.

(**MR. BEAUMONT** *'s smile drops. Brief silence.*)

I think we understand each other.

(**MR. BEAUMONT** *nods. Seconds later,* **MRS BEAUMONT** *enters from the front door. She hangs up the large pair of pruning shears next to the front door, takes her gloves off and mops her brow. She smiles.*)

MRS. BEAUMONT. Look at you two! Thick as thieves.

MR. BEAUMONT. A little warm out there, honey?

MRS. BEAUMONT. Just a little, angel bear. *(She composes herself)* Did you give the young man what he came for?

MR. BEAUMONT. I sure did. Great service they have at his place, don't you think?

MRS. BEAUMONT. Great service.

MR. BEAUMONT. Great service. I was just going to ask young Washington here whether he wanted to move in to the guest house.

(A beat)

MRS. BEAUMONT. What a good idea.

MR. BEAUMONT. It's a great idea.

MRS. BEAUMONT. It's a great idea. More the merrier.

MR. BEAUMONT. That's exactly what I thought when I first thought about inviting him to live in the guest house. "More the Merrier". What'd you say, Washington?

WASHINGTON. I ...accept.

MRS. BEAUMONT. That's settled then.

MR. BEAUMONT. It's a done deal.

WASHINGTON. I would need to get my things.

MR. BEAUMONT. I have an SUV.

MRS. BEAUMONT. He has an SUV. We could all get in it and go to the place where you keep your things.

MR. BEAUMONT. Get everything together, throw it in the back of the SUV and drive back here.

MRS. BEAUMONT. Oh how exciting.

MR. BEAUMONT. It's gonna be awesome.

(Silence)

WASHINGTON. So...when do you want ...

MRS. BEAUMONT. Yes. When do we want to do this?

MR. BEAUMONT. Later.

MRS. BEAUMONT. *(To WASHINGTON)* Later, honey.

WASHINGTON. Later?

MR. BEAUMONT. After golf.

MRS. BEAUMONT. That's right. After golf.

MR. BEAUMONT. Sunday's golf.

WASHINGTON. But… I don't play.

> *(**MR.** BEAUMONT *and* **MRS.** BEAUMONT *laugh.*)*

MRS. BEAUMONT. Oh baby, you're not going with him. I don't even get to go.

MR. BEAUMONT. She doesn't even get to go. You stay here.

MRS. BEAUMONT. We both stay here while he goes to golf.

MR. BEAUMONT. We'll get your things later.

MRS. BEAUMONT. Yes.

MR. BEAUMONT. "I don't play". That's gold. Pure gold. I'm going to like you, Washington. I can tell that already!

> *(**MR.** BEAUMONT *exits still laughing. After a couple of seconds,* **MRS.** BEAUMONT *stops laughing. Silence.*)*

MRS. BEAUMONT. So…good, *(almost singing it)* we have a guest for the guest house.

WASHINGTON. *(Laughs briefly)* Yes.

MRS BEAUMONT. Do you want to see it?

WASHINGTON. No, thank you. I'm sure it's great. You should sit down. You look tired.

MRS. BEAUMONT. *(Mockingly seductive)* Oh. Why, thank you…

WASHINGTON. Washington.

MRS. BEAUMONT. Why, thank you, Washington. I may just do that.

> *(She lies down on the sofa, facing* **WASHINGTON**. *She unbuttons a couple of buttons of her blouse and blows down her bra and then stares straight up at the ceiling and closes her eyes.)*

Oooohhh…fuck.

WASHINGTON. It is warm out there.

MRS. BEAUMONT. Yes. It. Is.

WASHINGTON. How's the pruning?

MRS. BEAUMONT. Oh, it's a pain. Such…beauty, surrounded by all this…yuck.

(She sits up briefly looks at WASHINGTON *who smiles at her. She lies back down again, closing her eyes once more.)*

I can't believe he let you smoke in here. He must like you. Just don't use the silver whatsit. That's his mother.

WASHINGTON. Yeah, no, he said. I just used this little plate.

(He lifts up the little plate to show her but she is not looking. Silence.)

MRS. BEAUMONT. So did you come to some arrangement?

WASHINGTON. What?

MRS. BEAUMONT. With my husband. To stay with us. He's… *(yawns)*…he's always making arrangements. Cutting deals. It's really quite funny.

(Pause)

WASHINGTON. I think we did, yes.

MRS. BEAUMONT. Huh?

WASHINGTON. Yes. We came to an arrangement.

MRS BEAUMONT. (Sleepily) Good …

(Silence. MRS. BEAUMONT *is dozing.* WASHINGTON *watches her.)*

Scene Two

(**WASHINGTON** *stands behind the sofa and over* **MRS.**
BEAUMONT *watching her sleep. The phone rings,*
WASHINGTON *dashes back to the armchair.* **MRS.**
BEAUMONT *wakes, but she remains still. It rings three*
or four more times and stops.)

MRS. BEAUMONT. *(Opening her eyes)* I'm sorry. I was dozing.
You must think I'm so rude.

WASHINGTON. You're fine.

MRS. BEAUMONT. I was dreaming.

WASHINGTON. You were?

MRS. BEAUMONT. Yes.

WASHINGTON. You weren't asleep for long.

MRS. BEAUMONT. It was a short dream. Have you ever
thought about suicide?

WASHINGTON. Is that what your dream was about?

MRS. BEAUMONT. No. But have you?

WASHINGTON. Sometimes.

MRS. BEAUMONT. How would you do it if you were going
to?

(There is a knock at the front door. **MRS BEAUMONT**
gets up, buttons up her blouse, straightens her hair and
walks over towards the front door. More knocking.)

We do have a door bell. Suicide, mmmh. We could do
it together.

*(**MRS. BEAUMONT** opens the front door to **AMBER**.*
WASHINGTON *stands.*)

Good afternoon.

AMBER. Just thought I'd drop by and say hi. *(A beat)* Are you finished with my blender?

*(**AMBER** enters and sees **WASHINGTON**. She looks him up and down.)*

MRS. BEAUMONT. Yes, you can take it back. I got a new one.

AMBER. Who's this?

MRS. BEAUMONT. Amber this is Washington. He's going to be staying with us for a while. Washington this is Amber from across the street. She and her husband, Todd are friends of ours.

*(Silence as **AMBER** looks at **WASHINGTON** curiously. She crosses to **WASHINGTON** and they shake hands.)*

AMBER. Very pleased to meet you …

WASHINGTON. Washington.

AMBER. Washington. How precious. *(To **MRS. BEAUMONT**)* Are you two alone?

MRS. BEAUMONT. No *(pointing upwards)* Daniel's getting ready.

AMBER. Is your Dad golfing too?

MRS. BEAUMONT. He should be here any minute.

AMBER. His back's okay?

MRS. BEAUMONT. I guess so.

*(**AMBER** sniffs for something.)*

AMBER. Has somebody been smoking in here?

WASHINGTON. Yeah. I just had one. You want one?

AMBER. No, it's quite alright. You keep them all for yourself, honey. *(To **MRS. BEAUMONT**)* I'm surprised you let him have a cigarette in here. It makes everything smell so disgusting.

MRS. BEAUMONT. It wasn't me. I was outside. *(To **WASHINGTON**)* Really, I don't mind.

AMBER. Well, I can't believe that. Daniel hates smokers. It had to be you.

MRS. BEAUMONT. No, really-

AMBER. You never want your home to smell disgusting. You don't want that at all.

WASHINGTON. No, it *was* actually Mr.-

MRS. BEAUMONT. *(Interrupting)* Amber, how is Todd doing?

AMBER. *(Defensively)* He's washing the car. Why do you ask?

MRS BEAUMONT. Er…no reason. Just…asking. We didn't see him with you in church today, that's all.

AMBER. He's fine. Washing the car, you know.

MRS. BEAUMONT. Yes.

AMBER. *(Distracted)* He's out of town again tomorrow. He needed to get ready for that. What ever is Daniel doing up there?

(Silence)

MRS. BEAUMONT. Well… I think I'm going to make myself a martini. Would anyone like to join me?

WASHINGTON. That'd be great.

MRS. BEAUMONT. Good. Amber?

AMBER. *(To* **WASHINGTON***)* How old are you?

WASHINGTON. I'm nineteen.

MRS. BEAUMONT. I'm sure one won't-

WASHINGTON. *(To* **MRS. BEAUMONT***)* It's okay. Seriously. Maybe not.

MRS. BEAUMONT. Okay. If you're sure. Amber? Martini?

AMBER. No, thanks.

MRS. BEAUMONT. Oh you'll have one if I make it. You always do.

AMBER. *(Firmly)* No. I won't.

(**MRS. BEAUMONT** *turns around and looks back at* **AMBER.***)*

AMBER. *(Carefully)* I won't, honey. So you would be just wasting your time making me one. And I don't really think you should be having one either. *(A beat)* I don't know what has got into you today, I really don't *(A beat)* I mean, I come over here and the lounge smells of cigarettes and you have this...boy, loitering about the place and Daniel's upstairs probably looking for something he needs for golf. Searching, here, there and everywhere, on his own, and you're asking everybody to join you for a martini. It's just not...right.

(MRS. BEAUMONT smiles politely at both AMBER and WASHINGTON and exits. Silence.)

AMBER. I just don't think that it's right, that's all.

(Seconds later, MR. BEAUMONT enters dressed for golfing and carrying his golf bag. He stops short when he sees AMBER and is clearly surprised to see her.)

MR. BEAUMONT. Amber.

AMBER. Daniel.

(Pause)

MR. BEAUMONT. I...uh, take it you and Washington introduced yourselves to each other.

AMBER. Oh...yes. Yes, we have.

MR. BEAUMONT. Good.

(Pause)

Washington is going to be staying with us for a while. In the guest house.

AMBER. So I hear.

MR. BEAUMONT. Uh...yeah. Should be lots of fun. Hey, Chief?

WASHINGTON. Lots of fun.

MR. BEAUMONT. Yeah.

(An awkward silence. There is a knock at the door. MR. BEAUMONT seems to welcome the interruption and goes over to open the front door to JACK who is also dressed for golf.)

JACK. Are you ready?

MR. BEAUMONT. Hi Jack.

(JACK enters like he owns the place. He playfully punches MR. BEAUMONT on the arm.)

JACK. Amber.

AMBER. Hello Jack. Nice to see you back on your feet again.

JACK. Are you kidding? Nothing's gonna keep me down for too long. I'm young, I'm strong, I'm virile. *(He sees* **WASHINGTON***)* What the hell's the kid from the video store doing here?

MR. BEAUMONT. Jack, this is Washington. He's going to be staying with us for a while.

AMBER. He's from the video store?

*(***MRS. BEAUMONT*** enters with two martinis)*

MRS. BEAUMONT. Daddy.

JACK. Washington? *(Abruptly to* **MRS. BEAUMONT***)* Is this one of your dumb ideas?

*(***MRS. BEAUMONT*** puts a martini into the hands of* **AMBER***.)*

MRS. BEAUMONT. *(To* **WASHINGTON***)* Washington, this is my father. Daddy, Washington is going to be-

JACK. Staying here for a while. Yeah, why?

(No response)

(Suddenly, with disbelief) Has someone been *smoking* in here?

WASHINGTON. Yes. That was me. I had a cigarette just a few minutes ago. You want one?

JACK. Am I even *awake?* Can somebody pinch me right now?

MR. BEAUMONT. Jack.

JACK. So what's the story?

(No response)

So?

WASHINGTON. Mr. and Mrs. Beaumont had rented a couple of movies.

JACK. And?

WASHINGTON. They were late bringing them back. So I came by to get them.

JACK. You came by?

WASHINGTON. So they wouldn't have to pay a fine.

JACK. And now you're *moving in*?

WASHINGTON. So it seems.

JACK. "So it seems". We've got a smart one here. Do I know your mom and dad?

WASHINGTON. It's unlikely. They gave me up when I was young.

MRS. BEAUMONT. Oh, honey.

JACK. I'm not surprised with a mouth like yours.

MRS. BEAUMONT. Daddy!

WASHINGTON. I was very young.

JACK. My daughter always did have a soft spot for stray puppies. She takes after her mother. But she's since moved on.

MR. BEAUMONT. It's okay, Jack.

JACK. It'd better. I love you like you're my blood, Daniel, you know that. But you need to keep this wife of yours in check.

MR. BEAUMONT. I will.

JACK. *(To* **WASHINGTON***)* And you better keep that place in good shape, you hear me? I built that thing with my own bare hands. Well not literally, I didn't build it, I paid for it...loaned Daniel here the money...loaned him half and he paid me back. *(A beat)* Now you just take care of it or I'll skin you alive. You got that?

WASHINGTON. I certainly will, sir.

JACK. Good because I'll have my eyes on you. You'd better get used to that. *(Puts out his hand to shake,* **WASHINGTON** *takes it.)* Jack.

(Silence)

MR. BEAUMONT. Honey, what are you drinking?

MRS. BEAUMONT. A martini.

JACK. *(Erupting)* What are you, an alcoholic now? *(To* **MR. BEAUMONT***)* Come on Daniel, step it up, guy! I'm out of action for a couple of weeks and I come back to *this*!

MR. BEAUMONT. Pour it out. *(A beat)* Amber does not look like she wants hers either.

AMBER. Thank you, Daniel.

> *(***MRS. BEAUMONT** *does not move.)*

MR. BEAUMONT. Darling?

MRS. BEAUMONT. Yes, honey.

MR. BEAUMONT. Take the drinks back into the kitchen and pour them out.

> *(Pause)*

MRS. BEAUMONT. Of course.

> *(***MRS. BEAUMONT** *walks over to* **AMBER.** **AMBER** *hands her the martini.* **MRS. BEAUMONT** *takes both glasses and exits through the door leading to the rest of the house.)*

JACK. I need ice for my water. It's hotter than a whore in hell out there.

> *(***JACK** *follows* **MRS. BEAUMONT.** *Awkward silence as* **MR. BEAUMONT, AMBER** *and* **WASHINGTON** *are left alone.)*

MR. BEAUMONT. Washington, can you go help Jack with the ice.

WASHINGTON. He doesn't know where you keep it?

> *(A beat)*

MR. BEAUMONT. Please.

> *(***WASHINGTON** *exits through the door leading to the rest of the house.)*

MR. BEAUMONT. What are you doing?

AMBER. I'm making brownies. Almonds or chocolate chip?

MR. BEAUMONT. Are you serious?

AMBER. Daniel.

MR. BEAUMONT. *(Flustered slightly)* I don't know. I love whatever you make. Chocolate chip, whatever.

AMBER. What's wrong? *(A beat)* Who is this boy?

(WASHINGTON re-enters.)

WASHINGTON. He found where you keep the ice.

(AMBER stares at MR. BEAUMONT for a moment then exits the front door. WASHINGTON stares at MR. BEAUMONT quizzically.)

MR. BEAUMONT. What?

(JACK, holding a plastic cup and MRS. BEAUMONT enter.)

JACK. Let's get this show on the road.

MR. BEAUMONT. Ready when you are, Jack.

MRS. BEAUMONT. Where did Amber go?

MR. BEAUMONT. Uh, she just left. I don't know.

MRS. BEAUMONT. She didn't take her blender.

MR BEAUMONT *(To WASHINGTON)* We'll go get your things when I get back.

WASHINGTON. Right.

JACK. *(Patting MR. BEAUMONT on the back)* I'm re-charged, Danny Boy! You don't know what you're getting yourself into!

(MR. BEAUMONT and JACK exit out the front door. Brief silence.)

MRS. BEAUMONT. I'm going to have a martini. Can I get you anything? A sandwich maybe? How about a soda?

WASHINGTON. No, thank you, Mrs. Beaumont.

(Silence. MRS. BEAUMONT smiles at WASHINGTON who smiles back. MRS. BEAUMONT exits through the door leading to the rest of the house. WASHINGTON lights up a cigarette and begins to smoke. He takes the arm chair, reaches over next to him, picks up the urn and takes the lid off and rests the urn on his lap. Lights fade.)

Scene Three

(Late night/early morning. Dimly lit. **MR. BEAUMONT** *has just finished fucking* **AMBER** *who is bent over the back of the sofa.* **MR. BEAUMONT** *is wearing a letterman jacket,* **AMBER** *is dressed in a cheerleader's uniform. They each gather their breath.* **MR. BEAUMONT** *moves away from her and zips up his fly. Unlike* **AMBER**, *he has been drinking for most of the night.* **AMBER**, *pulls her pants up and adjusts her skirt. There is a slight post-coital embarrassment between the two. They smile, shake their heads, laugh briefly etc.)*

AMBER. Do you love me?

MR. BEAUMONT. Of course. *(A beat)* What?

AMBER. Nothing.

MR. BEAUMONT. Sure I do. Does it not look like I do?

AMBER. No…

MR. BEAUMONT. No?

AMBER. No, I mean, yes. You do, I just…it doesn't matter. *(A beat)* Are you drunk?

MR. BEAUMONT. Nah. Just…full. Too much beer. You didn't drink anything tonight.

AMBER. I didn't feel like it.

MR. BEAUMONT. You okay?

AMBER. Yeah *(A beat)* Are you going to go back and get her?

MR. BEAUMONT. I don't know. What do you think?

AMBER. If she's not back soon then maybe you should.

MR. BEAUMONT. She'll be fine.

AMBER. She's pretty drunk.

MR. BEAUMONT. Yeah.

AMBER. For a change.

(Silence)

AMBER. You think Wellington heard anything? Us...?

MR. BEAUMONT. Washington?

AMBER. Whatever.

MR. BEAUMONT. Nah.

AMBER. Does he even have any friends?

MR. BEAUMONT. Not sure. Kinda keeps himself to himself.

AMBER. It's so weird.

MR. BEAUMONT. What?

AMBER. Him staying here.

MR. BEAUMONT. Why?

AMBER. He's like the weird kid in high school.

MR. BEAUMONT. *(Considers for a moment)* Yeah, I don't know, I kind of like that about him.

(Pause)

MR. BEAUMONT. What is it with Brent and his hot tub?

AMBER. Seriously.

MR. BEAUMONT. You haven't even been there ten minutes and he's asking you whether you need shorts for later. It's like, dude, can I get a Corona first?

AMBER. And she's just the same. *(A beat)* Did you feel her tits?

MR. BEAUMONT. Yeah.

AMBER. Almost five years and everyone still has to feel her tits.

MR. BEAUMONT. They sure love that hot tub.

AMBER. Do you think it's because they're from Alaska?

MR. BEAUMONT. I think it's because he wants to fuck my wife.

AMBER. Really?

MR. BEAUMONT. Tonight, he did. He fucking wouldn't leave her alone.

AMBER. Does that bother you?

MR. BEAUMONT. No, but it's the principle. I'm right there.

AMBER. Todd says he always sees his brother at the gym. He thinks he's on steroids.

MR. BEAUMONT. Jeez, you think. He's always been a jerk. His kids are assholes too.

(**AMBER** *laughs*)

AMBER. Daniel.

MR. BEAUMONT. What?

AMBER. They're eight years old.

MR. BEAUMONT. So? They are. And I just don't like identical twins.

AMBER. Now you're being ridiculous.

MR. BEAUMONT. What, it creeps me out. It's like two of them, exactly the same, always whispering some secret twin code to each other, getting all bent out of shape when you call one by the other's name like you're supposed to be psychic...don't even get me started on triplets.

AMBER. You don't know any triplets. And not all twins are like that.

MR. BEAUMONT. Well, theirs are. They came joined our table at *Olive Garden* once and I swear, Jesus.

AMBER. Well, I'm glad we're not having twins.

MR. BEAUMONT. I'm getting a drink. Do you want a drink?

(**MR. BEAUMONT** *gets up from the sofa and walks over the door leading to the rest of the house.*)

AMBER. What, you didn't hear me?

MR. BEAUMONT. Huh?

AMBER. I'm pregnant.

MR. BEAUMONT. *(Chuckles)* From just now? Give it some time. That's not quite how it works.

AMBER. Daniel. I'm serious.

(**MR. BEAUMONT** *stops. Silence.*)

I'm pregnant.

MR. BEAUMONT. How?

AMBER. I don't know, I guess…what I was on isn't, you know, 100% …

MR. BEAUMONT. Wow. *(A beat)* You're positive?

AMBER. I've seen a doctor.

MR. BEAUMONT. Wow. I mean…wow. *(Pause)* And it's mine?

(She gives him a look.)

MR. BEAUMONT. It's mine. Wow. *(A beat)* Why didn't you tell me earlier?

AMBER. I was scared to…and I just didn't know for sure . . .

MR. BEAUMONT. It doesn't matter. Fuck …

AMBER. I know. I didn't think I wanted this…not right now, obviously, and when I knew there was a possibility I was…well… I thought it was the worst thing to have happened, just the worst thing, but….

MR. BEAUMONT. But?

AMBER. But it's *ours.*

(Pause)

MR. BEAUMONT. So how long?

AMBER. Seven weeks.

MR. BEAUMONT. You think it's a boy?

AMBER. *(Laughs briefly)* Daniel.

MR. BEAUMONT. I've always wanted a boy.

(Silence. They smile at each other)

MR. BEAUMONT. I love you.

AMBER. You do?

MR. BEAUMONT. Yes. I love you.

AMBER. I love you.

(They embrace, kiss and hold each other. Silence)

MR. BEAUMONT. How the hell are we going to keep a secret like this?

AMBER. I'll leave him. I won't ask for anything. Just a divorce, no settlement or anything. Things should go fast, right?

(He breaks away from her)

AMBER. Daniel?

MR. BEAUMONT. I … I can't do that.

AMBER. Here we go.

MR. BEAUMONT. What?

AMBER. You're freaking out.

MR. BEAUMONT. But, I can't, I can't do that.

AMBER. What?

MR. BEAUMONT. Not right now.

AMBER. What are you talking about?

MR. BEAUMONT. I…well… I just can't afford it. Not right now.

AMBER. What do you mean?

MR. BEAUMONT. I can't afford a divorce. Not from her. She'll finish me.

AMBER. Why? Where else did you think this was headed between you and I? *(A beat)* It might be a little tight at first. But…you do well, don't you? *(A beat)* Daniel?

MR. BEAUMONT. It's just…things at the moment, they're getting a little tight, the business, there's just been a real downturn… I'm sure it's a phase, just the current climate, you know.

AMBER. So you want me to get rid of it?

MR. BEAUMONT. No. No way!

AMBER. Well I guess that's something.

(Pause)

I'm not going to live in an apartment, Daniel. Or some trailer. Not with a baby.

(Silence)

Well you need to work something out. Will you work something out? *(A beat)* Will you?

MR. BEAUMONT. Yeah… I…

AMBER. Daniel. Promise me.

MR. BEAUMONT. Yes.

(**WASHINGTON** *enters from the door leading to the rest of the house. He wears pajama bottoms, socks and a tee-shirt. He's also wearing glasses. There is nothing unusual about them.*)

WASHINGTON. How was the costume party?

MR. BEAUMONT. Hey, there he is! You're up! And what the *fuck* are you wearing?

WASHINGTON. What?

MR. BEAUMONT. On your eyes.

WASHINGTON. Oh. I wear glasses sometimes. On my nose. Keeps them up.

MR. BEAUMONT. *(To* **AMBER***)* Didn't I tell you? He's a fucking riot.

AMBER. You look so odd in them.

WASHINGTON. Hello, Amber. Pleasant evening? *(Does not wait for an answer. To* **MR. BEAUMONT***)*

Where's Mrs. Beaumont?

MR. BEAUMONT. She's still at the party. We couldn't drag her away. How was your night?

WASHINGTON. Fell asleep watching TV.

MR. BEAUMONT. Awesome. I love it when that happens. I'm getting a drink. You want one?

AMBER. Daniel.

WASHINGTON. Sure.

(**MR. BEAUMONT** *exits the door leading to the rest of the house.* **WASHINGTON** *goes over and sits on the armchair.* **AMBER** *watches him, clearly irritated by his presence. Every now and then during the following there are sounds of* **MR. BEAUMONT** *clattering about in the kitchen, the clinking of glasses, utensils being dropped, ice being crushed etc.*)

We were talking.

WASHINGTON. Oh. Anything I can help you with?

(Silence. **AMBER** *goes over to the sofa and sits.)*

WASHINGTON. Where's Todd tonight?

AMBER. Todd?

WASHINGTON. Your husband?

AMBER. He's away. He's back tomorrow.

(Silence)

WASHINGTON. So, any anecdotes?

AMBER. What?

WASHINGTON. Anecdotes. Stories.

AMBER. I know what an anecdote is.

WASHINGTON. You do?

AMBER. Don't talk to me like I'm stupid. You don't know anything about me.

(Pause)

WASHINGTON. Okay.

*(**WASHINGTON** picks up a golf magazine from nearby and starts to flip through it.)*

AMBER. Anecdotes about what?

WASHINGTON. The party. Any gossip? There's always something that goes down at a party. Any gossip?

AMBER. No. Just a party with friends and neighbors. We're a close knit community here.

WASHINGTON. Right.

(Silence)

AMBER. You must like staying here.

WASHINGTON. Better than my old place, that's for sure.

AMBER. I bet.

WASHINGTON. Yeah, you know, just the usual…room mate stuff. You know how it is.

AMBER. Room mate stuff?

WASHINGTON. Yeah, he's a cutter. Got a bit much at times.

AMBER. A cutter?

WASHINGTON. You know, slashes himself every now and then. On his arms. With a knife. On purpose.

AMBER. He sounds precious.

(**WASHINGTON** *discards the magazine.*)

WASHINGTON. Todd goes away a lot.

AMBER. Just for the time being. His company is in the middle of a merger. He's involved in that.

WASHINGTON. Do you ever wonder about that? I guess, it's kind of cliché. What he's doing. Who he's with.

AMBER. No. Why should I?

WASHINGTON. No reason. You're a better person than me.

AMBER. We have a trusting marriage.

WASHINGTON. That's nice. That's important. I always think people are up to something.

AMBER. That's paranoia.

WASHINGTON. Curiosity. I'm a curious cat. Curiosity killed the cat.

AMBER. It did.

WASHINGTON. I've always wanted to invent a saying or proverb. Like "Curiosity killed the cat" but just one that doesn't make sense, you know? A complete bullshit saying, but it sounds like it means something. But the thing is about this saying is that it catches on like wild fire and suddenly everyone starts saying it.

AMBER. Well, why don't you?

WASHINGTON. I might. What about kids?

AMBER. What about them?

WASHINGTON. Has to be the next step, right? I mean, you certainly have the set up. You all do around here. It's like something you see on TV. I'd have loved to grow up in a place like this when I was a kid.

AMBER. Oh, that's right. Your parents didn't want you.

WASHINGTON. Yes. That's right. They didn't.

(*A beat*)

So were you a cheerleader in high school?

AMBER. Is he supporting you while you live here?

WASHINGTON. Who? Mr. Beaumont?

AMBER. Yes.

WASHINGTON. I'm not sure that's any of your business.

AMBER. Excuse me?

(Pause)

WASHINGTON. He's just helping me out. Until I go work for him at his place.

AMBER. What about the video store?

WASHINGTON. Oh, I quit.

AMBER. You quit?

WASHINGTON. Yeah, it just wasn't practical. Time to move on. "Expand the Brand" as Mr. Beaumont says. I can see myself living in a place like this in the future. I'm not going to be able to do that working at a video store. How much does Todd earn annually?

AMBER. I'm not telling you that.

WASHINGTON. Ballpark figure.

AMBER. No.

WASHINGTON. See, I was on eight bucks an hour at the video store. I can't own a place like this on that.

AMBER. Probably not.

WASHINGTON. Still, it wasn't without its perks.

AMBER. The video store.

WASHINGTON. Sure.

AMBER. All the ice cream?

WASHINGTON. All the movies I got to see. I really watched a bunch. Lately, I've developed an interest in foreign film. Have yourself and Todd traveled extensively?

AMBER. I don't know…we've been to Hawaii, Mexico, we went to Paris a couple of years ago.

WASHINGTON. See if I was in your position I'd travel extensively. With your status. They say it broadens the mind and I totally get that. I've been to France, Brazil, the UK, Italy, Australia, you name it, just by watching movies. I'd love to go for real.

(**AMBER** *laughs*)

WASHINGTON. What?

AMBER. Why are you such a freak?

WASHINGTON. Why am I a freak?

AMBER. I don't know. Just the way you talk sometimes. I'm not being rude. You just sound like a freak.

WASHINGTON. I don't think so.

AMBER. Well, whatever. Maybe not.

WASHINGTON. I just said that you can learn things from watching movies, and that some of you around here could spend your money in a better way, that's all.

AMBER. You sound bitter about it.

WASHINGTON. I'm not bitter.

AMBER. Jealous?

(The phone rings. **WASHINGTON** *and* **AMBER** *remain seated. It rings three or four more times and stops.* **MR. BEAUMONT** *enters from the door leading to the rest of the house. He looks over at the phone. He's holding a bottle of vodka that he's obviously been drinking from.)*

MR. BEAUMONT. Coming right up. You two okay?

WASHINGTON. Yeah, we're getting on great.

AMBER. Washington here doesn't think we know how to spend our money, he thinks we should travel more.

MR. BEAUMONT. Not a bad idea. The French are assholes. Back in a sec.

*(***MR BEAUMONT*** *exits the door leading to the rest of the house)*

WASHINGTON. Maybe, you're the one who's jealous.

AMBER. Of what, Wellington?

WASHINGTON. Washington. You tell me.

AMBER. Why would I be jealous of you?

WASHINGTON. I don't know. Why would you?

(Silence)

AMBER. Don't get too comfortable here.

WASHINGTON. Why's that?

AMBER. Just don't. If you take advantage of him you won't know what's hit you.

WASHINGTON. Is that a threat?

AMBER. No. Just…a warning.

WASHINGTON. Of what?

AMBER. You're out of your league here.

*(****MR. BEAUMONT*** *enters from the door leading to the rest of the house. He is carrying two drinks in large cocktail glasses.)*

MR. BEAUMONT. Drinks! Now I think I've fucked these up.

*(****MR. BEAUMONT*** *hands* **WASHINGTON** *his drink and he joins* **AMBER** *on the sofa.)*

WASHINGTON. What is it?

MR. BEAUMONT. A kind of *Long Island Margarita Iced Tea Mojito.* Try it. So what are we talking about?

AMBER. Washington and I were just discussing World Cinema.

MR. BEAUMONT. World Cinema, huh?

AMBER. *(Without irony)* Washington was saying that when he watches a film from one of the great foreign directors he is being invited to feel, whereas with Hollywood he thinks he is being treated more as a consumer. It was an interesting insight.

(Silence. **MR. BEAUMONT** *looks blankly at* **WASHINGTON** *and* **AMBER***)*

MR. BEAUMONT. Jeez, I'm sorry I missed it.

(Long silence. **MR. BEAUMONT** *gets up from the sofa.)*

MR. BEAUMONT. Music?

AMBER. I best be going.

*(****MR. BEAUMONT*** *sits back down.)*

MR. BEAUMONT. No, stay a while. We're just getting started.

*(****AMBER*** *gets up.)*

AMBER. No, really. It's late. Can you walk me home?

WASHINGTON. It's across the street.

MR. BEAUMONT. You always walk a lady home, Washington. *(To* AMBER*)* You don't want to stay until I finish my drink?

(No response)

I guess not.

AMBER. Good night.

WASHINGTON. Good night, Amber.

(**MR. BEAUMONT** *sets his drink down, gets up, and walks* AMBER *to the door.)*

MR. BEAUMONT. *(To* WASHINGTON*)* Back in five.

(**MR. BEAUMONT** *and* AMBER *exit.)*

Scene Four

(**WASHINGTON** *is asleep in the armchair. There are sounds of movement from the kitchen that wake him up. He looks towards the door leading to the rest of the house and* **MRS**. **BEAUMONT** *enters. She is also dressed in a cheerleader's uniform. She has been drinking for most of the night. She stands in the doorway.*)

MRS. BEAUMONT. There you are.

WASHINGTON. Me?

MRS. BEAUMONT. Yes, you. Your light was on, so I came to say hi. But when I went in, you weren't there. I was like, where's Washy? But here you are.

WASHINGTON. Yep, I'm here. Did you have a good time?

MRS BEAUMONT. Meh. *(A beat)* What are you drinking?

WASHINGTON. I don't know, pesticide or something.

MRS. BEAUMONT. Can I have one?

(**MRS**. **BEAUMONT** *moves over to the sofa and sees the other drink.*)

MRS. BEAUMONT. Is this one for me?

WASHINGTON. *(Glancing over to the front door)* Uhm…sure.

MRS. BEAUMONT. *(Teasing)* Is this *really* for me? Is there somebody else?

WASHINGTON. *(Laughs nervously)* No. No, it's for you.

(**MRS**. **BEAUMONT** *takes a big sip of her drink.*)

MRS. BEAUMONT. God, that tastes like shit. What did you do tonight? I didn't know you wear glasses.

WASHINGTON. Yeah. Sometimes.

MRS. BEAUMONT. They look cute. I like 'em.

WASHINGTON. You do?

MRS. BEAUMONT. Why don't you have a girlfriend? You should have a girlfriend. What did you do tonight?

WASHINGTON. I just stayed in. Watched some TV. How was the party?

MRS. BEAUMONT. Desperate. Have you seen my husband?

WASHINGTON. I think he's walking Amber home or something.

MRS. BEAUMONT. That fucking bitch.

WASHINGTON. Yeah.

MRS. BEAUMONT. My husband.

(She laughs)

WASHINGTON. Oh right, yeah.

MRS. BEAUMONT. No she's a bitch too, I guess. I don't know, I don't think I've ever thought about it…robotic maybe…robotic bitch …

(She drinks)

He left me there. Who does that?

(She drinks. She sets the drink down and leans back into the sofa.)

WASHINGTON. How are you feeling?

MRS. BEAUMONT. I think I'm going to puke.

WASHINGTON. Do you want me to get you some water?

MRS. BEAUMONT. No, no. I should stop drinking. Don't you hate that? You get all hot and the room starts spinning and you're like "I am no longer in control of this situation".

*(***WASHINGTON*** gets up.)*

WASHINGTON. Let me get you some water.

MRS. BEAUMONT. No stay here and talk to me.

*(***WASHINGTON*** sits back down.)*

You haven't told me I look pretty.

WASHINGTON. Because you always do, Mrs. Beaumont.

MRS. BEAUMONT. I used to be skinnier.

WASHINGTON. I think you're just about perfect.

MRS. BEAUMONT. Awww. You're so sweet. Give me a hug. Come here...come here.

(WASHINGTON *stands and looks over at the front door.*)

No, wait. Do you have any cigarettes? I want a cigarette.

WASHINGTON. They're in my room.

MRS. BEAUMONT. I'm a married woman, Washington.

WASHINGTON. Oh no, I was just saying-

MRS. BEAUMONT. I'm fucking with you. Go and get them. We'll have one in here.

WASHINGTON. Are you sure?

MRS. BEAUMONT. Yeah. Go and get 'em.

WASHINGTON. But Mr. Beaumont-

MRS. BEAUMONT. If Mr. Beaumont says anything we'll fucking set him on fire. Go get 'em. Oh, and in the kitchen drawer, second one down...

WASHINGTON. Yeah?

MRS. BEAUMONT. Daddy's medication. Just take two. We'll have one each.

WASHINGTON. What are they?

MRS. BEAUMONT. Pain killers for his back. They're delicious.

(WASHINGTON *exits quickly through the door leading to the rest of the house.* MRS. BEAUMONT *is left alone on stage.* WASHINGTON *returns with the cigarettes and lighter and a glass of water. He looks over towards the front door.*)

Fantastic.

WASHINGTON. Here, drink this.

MRS. BEAUMONT. Did you get the pills?

WASHINGTON. You don't need those.

(*He hands her the glass of water which she downs in one. He takes the glass from her and sets it down. He hands*

her a cigarette and lights it for her. He lights himself a
cigarette. They smoke.)

MRS. BEAUMONT. So what did you do tonight?

WASHINGTON. Just watched TV.

MRS. BEAUMONT. Was there any sex and violence?

WASHINGTON. Uhm, I think a bit of both.

MRS. BEAUMONT. What a society. How do you like the guest
house? Are we being good hosts?

WASHINGTON. It's great. You've both been very kind.

MRS. BEAUMONT. Do you like my garden?

WASHINGTON. Out front?

MRS. BEAUMONT. Yes.

WASHINGTON. I … I do.

MRS. BEAUMONT. You can admit it. It won't make you less
of a boy to say that you like my garden.

WASHINGTON. Less of a man.

MRS. BEAUMONT. What?

WASHINGTON. It won't make me less of a man.

MRS. BEAUMONT. A young man.

WASHINGTON. That's fine. I'm just not a boy.

MRS. BEAUMONT. Well excuse me. It won't make you less of
a young man to say that you like my garden.

WASHINGTON. I like your garden, Mrs. Beaumont.

MRS. BEAUMONT. It needs pruning. Wouldn't it be nice if
life was like that. You could just prune away at things.
Anything that was ugly and nasty that stopped you
from growing or blossoming, you could just snip right
away.

WASHINGTON. That would be good.

MRS. BEAUMONT. But I guess that's the argument for ethnic
cleansing.

WASHINGTON. Maybe.

MRS. BEAUMONT. And that's awful.

WASHINGTON. What?

MRS. BEAUMONT. Ethnic cleansing.

WASHINGTON. Yeah, no. It's not nice.

MRS. BEAUMONT. I wasn't meaning it like that.

WASHINGTON. I didn't think you did. I know you didn't mean people.

MRS. BEAUMONT. Well, I was thinking of certain people when I said it actually. They're just not ethnic.

(She laughs)

WASHINGTON. *(Laughs briefly)* You're drunk.

MRS. BEAUMONT. A little. *(A beat)* We're all ethnic, what am I saying…

WASHINGTON. I know what you meant.

MRS. BEAUMONT. I can't believe he left me there. Who does that?

(Pause)

MRS. BEAUMONT. Is he in bed? Have you seen him tonight?

WASHINGTON. No, no… I haven't seen him.

MRS. BEAUMONT. Huh.

(Silence)

WASHINGTON. "Heroism is the fruit of all deliverance".

MRS. BEAUMONT. What?

WASHINGTON. It's a saying. A proverb.

MRS. BEAUMONT. No, it isn't.

WASHINGTON. You're right. I made it up.

MRS. BEAUMONT. Did you?

WASHINGTON. Yeah. It doesn't mean anything.

MRS. BEAUMONT. That's funny!

WASHINGTON. You think so?

MRS. BEAUMONT. When I was 17, I had a boyfriend, army brat, he was only here twelve months. We used to make up stuff like that and send them to each other, or write really bad love poetry to each other, on purpose… "Your sky wanders collidingly into my clouds of sorrow's wonder…and I am erect".

(No response)

MRS BEAUMONT. You had to be there really. *(A beat)* We were so funny together. He was such a goofball. It's funny how things… *(Pause)* I don't know… *(A beat)* You wouldn't do that would you, Washy?

WASHINGTON. What's that?

MRS. BEAUMONT. Leave your wife at a party.

WASHINGTON. Not if it was you.

MRS. BEAUMONT. Why, you are just the charmer tonight! I want to dance. Can you dance? I haven't had anyone to dance with all night.

WASHINGTON. Didn't you say you were going to puke?

MRS. BEAUMONT. Slow dancing and I feel fine now.

WASHINGTON. I don't really dance.

(She gets up and takes his hand.)

MRS. BEAUMONT. Come, have you ever danced with a cheerleader before?

WASHINGTON. No.

MRS. BEAUMONT. What about just a woman?

WASHINGTON. No, I don't think I have.

MRS. BEAUMONT. Well now we're definitely dancing.

WASHINGTON. I'm not a virgin.

MRS. BEAUMONT. Congratulations.

WASHINGTON. I'm not.

MRS. BEAUMONT. Mazel Tov. What's that got to do with anything?

WASHINGTON. I'm sorry… I don't know…it just seemed like you may think that.

MRS. BEAUMONT. Do you want to talk about your first sexual experience?

WASHINGTON. Not really.

MRS. BEAUMONT. Good. Neither do I. Come on. Up.

*(**WASHINGTON** stands up, he looks over at the front door. **MRS. BEAUMONT** takes **WASHINGTON** by hand to a space in the middle of the room.)*

MRS. BEAUMONT. Give me your hands.

*(**WASHINGTON** gives her his hands. She puts one on her shoulder and one on her waist. She puts her hand on his shoulder and one his waist.)*

WASHINGTON. What about music?

MRS. BEAUMONT. We don't need music.

*(**WASHINGTON** breaks away from her and goes over to the front door.)*

Come back. Where are you going?

WASHINGTON. Just a sec.

*(**WASHINGTON** opens the front door and looks around outside. He closes the door and goes back to **MRS. BEAUMONT**.)*

Okay.

(They revert back to their dancing positions.)

MRS. BEAUMONT. Just follow me.

*(They begin to waltz slowly. Both looking down at their feet initially. As they get into a rhythm and **WASHINGTON** relaxes, he gently spins her and pulls her in etc.)*

Do you have a song in your head?

WASHINGTON. Yeah.

MRS. BEAUMONT. What is it?

WASHINGTON. No... I don't... I don't know why I said that I did.

MRS. BEAUMONT. You're a good dancer.

WASHINGTON. Do you still think about killing yourself?

MRS. BEAUMONT. Why do you ask?

WASHINGTON. You told me you did. Do you?

MRS. BEAUMONT. When? Oh I remember, yes...often. You've done this before.

WASHINGTON. No, it's my first time. *(A beat)* You said you wanted to do it together.

(She rests her head on his shoulder, the dance gets slower and slower and the steps smaller and smaller to the point they are barely moving. They hold each other tighter and tighter and finally they are still. Silence.)

MRS. BEAUMONT. That was nice.

WASHINGTON. Yeah.

(She breaks away from him and smiles and touches his face.)

MRS. BEAUMONT. Washy, I'm…

WASHINGTON. What?

MRS. BEAUMONT. I'm going to go prune.

WASHINGTON. Okay.

*(**MRS. BEAUMONT** goes and takes the large pair of pruning shears that hang next to the front door. **MR. BEAUMONT** enters the front door briskly and collides into **MRS. BEAUMONT** who loses her balance and falls.)*

MR. BEAUMONT. Woah! You're back.

*(No response. **MRS. BEAUMONT** seems embarrassed. **MR. BEAUMONT** offers his hand to help her up.)*

Here.

MRS. BEAUMONT. Don't touch me.

MR. BEAUMONT. Honey.

*(**MRS. BEAUMONT** stands. **MR. BEAUMONT** puts out an arm to her. She snaps the pruning shears at him. He pulls his arm away, dodges and smacks her hard across the face. She stares back at her husband, glances over at **WASHINGTON** and exits the front door.)*

Honey, come to bed.

(No response)

Honey. It's late. What are you doing?

(Sounds of snipping can be heard)

Is she alright?

WASHINGTON. Yeah. Just a little drunk.

MR. BEAUMONT. Honey, I'm going to close the door now.

(No response. Sounds of snipping continue.)

I'm closing the door.

(He starts closing the door.)

It's closing…closing…

(He shuts the front door.)

Un-fucking-believable *(A beat)* I'm sorry you had to see that.

(Pause)

WASHINGTON. That was more than five minutes.

MR. BEAUMONT. What, you have a stopwatch or something?

WASHINGTON. As long as she got home safely, I guess.

MR. BEAUMONT. That's right.

*(**MR. BEAUMONT** goes over and gets his drink, he looks at the reduced amount, he looks over to the front door and looks at **WASHINGTON** who shrugs. He sits down in the armchair.)*

You know Washington, I'd really appreciate it if you didn't smoke in here.

WASHINGTON. I'm sorry.

MR. BEAUMONT. It fucking stinks. Jesus.

(Silence)

WASHINGTON. I'm sorry. *(A beat)* I'm going to go to bed.

MR. BEAUMONT. Hey, look…

WASHINGTON. What?

(Pause)

MR. BEAUMONT. I'm sorry.

WASHINGTON. No, I apologize. I won't do it again.

MR. BEAUMONT. Forget it.

(Pause)

Listen, Red?

WASHINGTON. Yeah?

MR. BEAUMONT. I want to do it. I'm serious. I want her gone.

(Silence)

What, are you deaf?

WASHINGTON. No.

(Silence)

MR. BEAUMONT. Well?

WASHINGTON. What, now?

MR. BEAUMONT. No, not right now, what's wrong with you?

WASHINGTON. Well I've never done this before!

MR. BEAUMONT. Will you keep your voice down? I'm serious. It's just not fantasy anymore. It's for real. Look, how hard can it be? I bet people do this all the time…all those missing people…just get your thinking cap on, because I'm telling you, I'm fucking ready to roll. Give it some real thought instead of jerking off in your room all day. You've got nothing to do.

WASHINGTON. I'm not jerking off and I have nothing to do because you said you would give me a job.

MR. BEAUMONT. I'm working that out. Jeez, what is it with everyone tonight?

(No response)

We're smart guys you and me, it just needs a plan. Look, I have a gun, everything, bullets, in my dad's old golf bag, silencer. That's not a problem. It's just what we do with her after. That's the key. *(A beat)* What?

WASHINGTON. I didn't know you had a gun.

MR. BEAUMONT. It's Jack's. He had a spare. I told him I wanted one. Just for protection *(A beat)* What?

WASHINGTON. Then your wife goes missing? His daughter. That doesn't look good.

MR. BEAUMONT. See, that's why I need you.

WASHINGTON. What do you mean?

MR. BEAUMONT. You think outside the box.

(No response)

Jack loves me anyway. Shit, it seems like he loves me more than he does her. We don't have to worry about Jack.

WASHINGTON. Killing somebody is easy. Gun or no gun. It's getting rid of the evidence.

MR. BEAUMONT. Touché.

WASHINGTON. What?

MR. BEAUMONT. Exactly. That's why I need you. Now your mind's working.

WASHINGTON. Right. *(A beat)* Have you not just considered a divorce?

*(**MR. BEAUMONT** stares at **WASHINGTON**.)*

MR. BEAUMONT. *(Ironically)* You know, I hadn't.

(Silence)

So will you help me? *(A beat)* I expect your co-operation. Why do you think you're here in the first place for Chrissake.

(Pause)

WASHINGTON. Sure. *(A beat)* I'll help you.

MR. BEAUMONT. Good.

*(**MR. BEAUMONT** exhales.)*

WASHINGTON. What?

MR. BEAUMONT. I like how we can be frank with each other. Tell it like it is, but there's still a mutual respect there. You know what I mean?

WASHINGTON. Yeah.

*(**MR. BEAUMONT** approaches **WASHINGTON**. **WASHINGTON** appears nervous.)*

MR. BEAUMONT. Come here...give your old man a hug.

*(**MR. BEAUMONT** hugs **WASHINGTON**, **WASHINGTON** tentatively hugs back.)*

(Chuckles) I'd make a good Dad, huh?

WASHINGTON. The best.

(Silence. **MR. BEAUMONT** *keeps* **WASHINGTON** *in a hug for the following.)*

MR. BEAUMONT. What do you think of Amber?

(Pause)

WASHINGTON. She's…nice.

MR. BEAUMONT. Do you mean that?

WASHINGTON. Yeah.

MR. BEAUMONT. I want you to like my friends. It's important to me.

WASHINGTON. Why, did she say anything?

MR. BEAUMONT. Not really.

WASHINGTON. Okay.

(They break)

MR. BEAUMONT. She just doesn't like you.

WASHINGTON. Oh.

MR. BEAUMONT. Thinks you're weird.

WASHINGTON. Sure.

MR. BEAUMONT. But, she's like that…women, you know… she just doesn't know you like I do. But, try a little harder in future. If you feel yourself being weird, reign it in a notch.

WASHINGTON. I'll try.

MR. BEAUMONT. For me.

WASHINGTON. I will.

MR. BEAUMONT. She's a good friend.

WASHINGTON. Sure.

MR. BEAUMONT. Anyway… I need to hit the hay. We've got church first thing. Do you want us to wake you up?

WASHINGTON. No, it's fine.

MR. BEAUMONT. Are you sure?

WASHINGTON. I don't believe in Jesus and I think God's a concept.

(Pause)

MR. BEAUMONT. Well, if you change your mind…

> (**MR. BEAUMONT** *begins to exit towards the door leading to the rest of the house. He stops short and turns around)*

Hey, Chief?

> (**MR. BEAUMONT** *chuckles.)*

WASHINGTON. What?

MR. BEAUMONT. Those glasses. I don't know, man. *(Stop chuckling)* Look, it'll be fine.

WASHINGTON. Right.

MR. BEAUMONT. It will.

WASHINGTON. Yep.

MR. BEAUMONT. Night.

> (**MR. BEAUMONT** *exits. Moments later,* **MRS. BEAUMONT** *enters through the front door. She has a chrysanthemum in one hand and the large pair of pruning shears in the other.)*

WASHINGTON. Hey.

MRS. BEAUMONT. Has he gone to bed?

> (**MRS. BEAUMONT** *hangs up the large pair of pruning shears next to the front door.)*

WASHINGTON. Ahm, yeah. Just this second…

> (**MRS BEAUMONT** *stands by the front door holding the chrysanthemum out to* **WASHINGTON.** *)*

What's that for?

MRS. BEAUMONT. It's for you.

(Pause)

WASHINGTON. Why? What for?

MRS. BEAUMONT. For taking care of me.

WASHINGTON. It was nothing. You shouldn't of.

MRS. BEAUMONT. It was lonely. It didn't really fit with all the others.

(Silence)

MRS. BEAUMONT & WASHINGTON. *(Simultaneously)* What…

(A beat)

Don't you want it?

WASHINGTON. Yeah. *(A beat)* Yes, I do.

MRS. BEAUMONT. Well come and get it.

*(***WASHINGTON*** does not move)*

Come on, Washy.

*(***WASHINGTON*** does not move)*

Come here…

*(***WASHINGTON*** slowly approaches **MRS BEAUMONT**. Lights fade.)*

Scene Five

(An afternoon. Just over a week later. **MR. BEAUMONT** *enters from the front door. He appears anxious, distressed. He has just come from a funeral and is dressed appropriately. He sits down on the sofa. He gets up from the sofa and exits through the door leading to the rest of the house.* **WASHINGTON** *enters from the front door. He wears exactly the same suit, shirt and tie that* **MR. BEAUMONT** *is wearing, as the two men had bought their outfits together. He waits, listening to see if anyone is home.* **MR. BEAUMONT** *re-enters with a bottle of scotch and a glass.)*

MR. BEAUMONT. *(Vacantly)* Hey.

WASHINGTON. Hi.

*(***MR. BEAUMONT** *sits back down on the sofa and pours himself a scotch, he downs it almost immediately and pours himself another.)*

MR. BEAUMONT. Where did you go?

WASHINGTON. Just for a walk around the block. I don't know anyone there, so...

MR. BEAUMONT. I guess not.

(Pause)

WASHINGTON. *(Without any great feeling)* It's all so tragic.

(No response)

Are you okay?

(No response.)

Nice service. Under the circumstances. Your Pastor seems cool.

MR. BEAUMONT. *(Again, vacantly)* Yeah. It was. He is.

WASHINGTON. That woman really sang the hell out of that song. Was that her sister?

MR. BEAUMONT. Huh?

WASHINGTON. The woman who sang the song. Was that her sister?

MR. BEAUMONT. Yeah.

WASHINGTON. I think that was the best version of "*Wind Beneath My Wings*" I've ever heard.

*(*MR. BEAUMONT *starts to cry but almost immediately stops as the front door opens and* MRS. BEAUMONT *appears in the doorway. She too is dressed for a funeral.)*

MRS. BEAUMONT. Are either of you coming back?

(No response)

Todd's downstairs toilet is overflowing. *(A beat)* As if he didn't have enough to deal with, poor guy. He still has the upstairs bathroom but there always seems to be a huge line. *(A beat)* The Van Sants have said that people are free to use theirs next door. *(A beat)* I said the same with ours. So we may get traffic. *(A beat)* Everything okay?

(No response)

Daniel?

*(*MR. BEAUMONT *does not turn around.* WASHINGTON *nods to* MRS. BEAUMONT. *She exits. Silence.* MR. BEAUMONT *drains his glass once more. He pours himself another and rests back in the sofa.)*

WASHINGTON. Are you alright?

MR. BEAUMONT. It's rough, you know?

WASHINGTON. Yeah.

(Silence)

MR. BEAUMONT. How's your suit?

WASHINGTON. Feels good. Yours?

MR. BEAUMONT. You get what you pay for. They do a great job there. No need to go to any place else.

(Silence)

MR. BEAUMONT. I'll get you back.

WASHINGTON. Yeah, no problem.

MR. BEAUMONT. Sorry about that. Fucking embarrassing. It's just a mix up. Just haven't had chance to straighten out with the credit card company...just a mix up.

WASHINGTON. Sure.

(Silence)

Yeah, but if you can, you know. I'm maxed out.

MR. BEAUMONT. No, sure.

WASHINGTON. There's no way I can pay that off.

MR. BEAUMONT. I promise.

(Pause)

MR. BEAUMONT. You're a standup guy, Washington.

WASHINGTON. Thanks.

MR. BEAUMONT. You know, I wish I could adopt you. I looked into the possibility. You know, something official.

WASHINGTON. I'm too old.

MR. BEAUMONT. I know. That's what I found out.

WASHINGTON. I could have told you that.

MR. BEAUMONT. I guess I was just thinking about something official, you know?

WASHINGTON. Yeah.

(Silence)

WASHINGTON. Even if that wasn't a factor...

MR. BEAUMONT. What?

(Pause)

WASHINGTON. Well, I was going to say. Even if that wasn't a factor, you'd have a better chance if Mrs. Beaumont isn't eliminated. They like couples.

(Silence. **MR. BEAUMONT** *starts to cry once more but again stops himself almost immediately. He drains his glass and pours himself another.)*

MR. BEAUMONT. What a fucking mess.

(Silence)

You know, Wash?

WASHINGTON. Yes?

MR. BEAUMONT. I don't think this is going to work out. I don't want to do it anymore. I think things need to get back to normal here. *(A beat)* And you living here... I'm not sure I'm going to need you here after all...

WASHINGTON. What?

MR. BEAUMONT. Everything's changed now.

WASHINGTON. How? Why?

(No response)

But you said-

MR. BEAUMONT. But when business is better maybe you can work for me. I could groom you. Show you the ropes.

WASHINGTON. *(Seething) Maybe?* I quit my job. I'm broke. You maxed my credit card on these fucking suits! I left my-

(The front door bursts open, **JACK** *enters dressed for a funeral but not quite the same as what* **MR. BEAUMONT** *and* **WASHINGTON** *are wearing. He walks over to the door leading to the rest of the house.)*

JACK. The line for the John over there is *epic!* Beautiful service, wasn't it? Outstanding. And the song? The sister? What a set of pipes! I've been wanting to ask her where'd she learn to sing like that but she's hasn't stopped bawling since they got back!

*(***JACK** *exits though the door leading to the rest of the house.)*

MR. BEAUMONT. I won't leave you high and dry.

WASHINGTON. *Oh no?* Nah, you're upset, you're just not thinking clearly. You don't mean what you're saying.

(No response)

We had a deal.

MR. BEAUMONT. It's different now.

(WASHINGTON *seems preoccupied with an avalanche of thoughts. A couple of seconds later the front door opens and* **MRS. BEAUMONT** *enters. She takes off her shoes.)*

MRS. BEAUMONT. Oh well I just can't stay there. Everyone's either too distressed to talk or they're bouncing up and down, looking over your shoulder seeing what the line for the bathroom is like. It's impossible to have a conversation.

MR. BEAUMONT. *(Irritated)* It's a wake, honey. Because Amber is *dead.* It's not a cocktail party.

(JACK *re-enters. He is zipping up his fly and fastening his belt.)*

JACK. Once all the dust settles, Todd needs to get himself some brand new toilets for both upstairs and down. Today isn't the day to put him straight but I hear he's got Drakes.

He needs to go with a couple of Carlyles. You can damn near flush your garbage down those things. *(A beat)* I did for a while. *(To* **MRS. BEAUMONT***)* Just after your mother died. It was a helluva time…

(Silence)

Here's a kicker, Todd told me that the autopsy showed Amber was seven weeks pregnant.

(MR. BEAUMONT *drains his drink.)*

MRS. BEAUMONT. You're joking. I can't believe it.

JACK. Neither can Todd, he had a vasectomy last April.

MRS. BEAUMONT. Oh, you'd feel awful.

JACK. You'd be on the phone to your surgeon.

MRS. BEAUMONT. I didn't think they even wanted children.

JACK. Are you jealous? What you'd give for some of those ovaries, huh?

(No response)

WASHINGTON. Well you don't think it was Todd, do you?

MRS. BEAUMONT. What?

WASHINGTON. He found out she was…you know-

JACK. Hey, you just watch how you speak of the dead or you'll be picking up your teeth with broken fingers.

MRS. BEAUMONT. Daddy.

WASHINGTON. *(Ignoring* JACK*)* I'm just saying, maybe Todd found out something and…bam.

MRS. BEAUMONT. Todd?

WASHINGTON. You have the motive right there.

JACK. What's this, *Columbo?* What do you think the police have been doing all this time, you nimrod? He was away. He has an alibi. He's Todd. Besides, he's a data analyst.

(Silence)

(Ruefully) One afternoon you're baking cakes, you're greasing your tray…then all of a sudden, some nincompoop sneaks up on you and cracks you over the head with an industrial 4 way crimper handle. Broad daylight. Senseless.

MRS. BEAUMONT. I never got the chance to return her blender.

JACK. I just hope they catch the bastard.

MRS. BEAUMONT. It's a nice one too.

JACK. What, the crimper?

MRS. BEAUMONT. No… *(More to herself)* the blender.

MR. BEAUMONT. *(Getting up suddenly)* I need a walk.

MRS. BEAUMONT. Are you going back?

MR. BEAUMONT. No.

MRS. BEAUMONT. Where are you going?

MR. BEAUMONT. I need some air.

JACK. I'll come with you.

MR. BEAUMONT. No, Jack. Really. I just want to be by myself.

JACK. You're not going outside looking like that. Not on your own.

(No response. MR. BEAUMONT exits the front door. JACK turns to MRS. BEAUMONT.)

(Urgently) I'll take care of *your* husband. You get back across the street and be a neighbor. Leave the kid here. This is a respectable neighbourhood. People talk. Get a sense of priority, for heaven's sake.

(JACK exits the front door. WASHINGTON and MRS. BEAUMONT are left alone.)

MRS. BEAUMONT. May I have a cigarette?

WASHINGTON. Uh...sure.

(WASHINGTON reaches into his jacket and pulls out two cigarettes and lights them both in his mouth. He passes one to MRS. BEAUMONT.)

MRS. BEAUMONT. Thank you.

(They smoke.)

(Matter of fact) I'm not, you know.

WASHINGTON. You're not what?

MRS. BEAUMONT. Infertile.

WASHINGTON. You're not?

MRS. BEAUMONT. You can tell men anything clinical related to your vaginal area and they'll believe you because it all sounds so confusing.

WASHINGTON. *(Considers for a moment)* I guess.

MRS. BEAUMONT. It's almost unfair.

(Pause)

He makes all the decisions but I made the important one. I couldn't think of anything worse than having a child with that monster. I wouldn't wish half of him in anyone. But, he's never pushed me for proof. Not really.

WASHINGTON. I don't understand why you married him.

MRS. BEAUMONT. Because he was cute and so was I.

WASHINGTON. That's it?

MRS. BEAUMONT. And he was charming. I was young. Prospects, security. Suddenly everything seemed sewn right up by just saying "Yes".

WASHINGTON. Right.

MRS. BEAUMONT. My Mom cried at the wedding because she knew how it would be. Daddy was ecstatic.

WASHINGTON. I don't like the way they talk to you. Either of them.

MRS. BEAUMONT. He still fucks me like he did in college. It's like rape but without the surprise. *(A beat)* Daniel, I mean.

WASHINGTON. Of course.

MRS. BEAUMONT. Thankfully it's just not so regular. His hands disgust me. Do they disgust you?

WASHINGTON. His hands?

MRS. BEAUMONT. You must have noticed. I could write a book on how disgusting his hands are. Fat fingers, with its mousy hair that…sprouts. The way his wedding ring strangles his wedding finger with that little bit of skin pushed up over it. The truth is…with Amber, I envy her. She was happy in this whole…this little world, she didn't know any better…and she was demolished in her own kitchen before she figured it out.

WASHINGTON. Bludgeoned.

MRS. BEAUMONT. What?

WASHINGTON. Bludgeoned. Just another word for, it doesn't matter…

MRS. BEAUMONT. All week, I've gone around the house and undone all the locks on the doors and windows just in the hope that there's a serial killer on the loose and I'm next.

WASHINGTON. I've noticed you've been baking a lot.

MRS. BEAUMONT. I'm hoping to lure him in. It could be his trademark, his fetish. They have those, don't they, killers? Fetishes? He may have one. Baking. I doubt it's a she.

WASHINGTON. No.

(Pause)

MRS. BEAUMONT. I like you, Washington. You've been a breath of fresh air.

WASHINGTON. *(Heartfelt)* I feel the same about you. Ever since I first saw you come into the video store-

MRS. BEAUMONT. *(She stands, not listening)* I should get back and be the good neighbor. Pay my respects to the lucky bitch. And she was *a* bitch, wasn't she?

WASHINGTON. I didn't care for what I saw.

(Silence)

MRS. BEAUMONT. Come here.

(WASHINGTON does not move.)

(Quieter, but more insistent) Come here.

(WASHINGTON stubs out his cigarette, stands up and approaches MRS. BEAUMONT. MRS. BEAUMONT gives him a long kiss on the lips, when WASHINGTON starts to kiss back, she breaks away from him.)

(As if nothing had just happened) I like you. You're good to talk to.

(MRS. BEAUMONT stubs out her cigarette, puts on her shoes and makes her way to the front door. WASHINGTON remains rooted to the spot. Pause.)

WASHINGTON. So why don't you just leave him?

(MRS. BEAUMONT stares at WASHINGTON who looks right back at her.)

MRS. BEAUMONT. And what would I do?

(No response. MRS. BEAUMONT exits the front door. WASHINGTON sits down on the sofa, reflects and changes his position to lying across the sofa. He takes

out another cigarette and lights it. He smokes. The front door opens and **JACK** *enters.* **WASHINGTON** *looks up to see who it is and nonchalantly continues to smoke.* **JACK** *stands in the doorway staring at* **WASHINGTON.** *Silence.)*

JACK. You've got some brass balls, kid.

WASHINGTON. How's Mr. B?

JACK. Mr. Beaumont wants to be left alone. I respected his wishes.

WASHINGTON. He told you that before you followed him.

(**JACK** *forces a smile. He closes the front door behind him and moves over to the armchair and sits.)*

JACK. So how are you doing, young man?

WASHINGTON. Good. How are you, Jack?

JACK. What do you want with my daughter?

WASHINGTON. Your daughter?

JACK. Yes.

WASHINGTON. Your one and only?

JACK. Yes.

WASHINGTON. That was a lucky guess. She may have had siblings. I don't think we ever discussed it. She *really* is your one and only.

JACK. I said she was.

WASHINGTON. Well especially since there's no longer a… what's your last name?

JACK. Don't fuck with me, Geronimo.

WASHINGTON. …no longer a Mrs. Whatever-your-last-name-is, to clean up after your mess. To scrub up your filth.

JACK. Now you better just watch what you say next or…

WASHINGTON. Or what? Knock my teeth out? Skin me alive? How's your back, Jack? You're a relic. You're just an old fucking asshole.

JACK. WHAT ARE YOU DOING HERE?

WASHINGTON. I LIVE HERE!

JACK. WHY?

WASHINGTON. THEY ASKED ME!

JACK. WHO?

WASHINGTON. BOTH OF THEM!

JACK. WHO ASKED FIRST?

(*No response*)

JACK. WHO INVITED YOU FIRST?

WASHINGTON. HE DID!

JACK. WHY?

(*No response*)

WHY?

(*No response*)

I could smell something wasn't right the day you first came in here. Some smelly little punk, sniffing around! I don't know what kind of yarn you've been spinning him all this time, but this little circus ends today!

WASHINGTON. This isn't your house.

(**JACK** *launches out of the armchair, slaps the cigarette from* **WASHINGTON** *and then pulls him off the sofa and throws him to the floor.* **JACK** *reaches for his back gingerly, feeling pain.* **WASHINGTON** *is visibly shaken.*)

JACK. He's a good, decent man. You're out of here, pal. They have a life together here and over my dead body are you going to mess with that. You stay away from my daughter!

WASHINGTON. *Good, decent man?* Ha! He's an animal! And he's been fucking that dead whore across the street since probably time began!

JACK. That's horse shit and I've already warned you about talking like that on a day like today. You've got no sense of decency?

WASHINGTON. Well he doesn't get to anymore! No sir! I made sure of that!

(**WASHINGTON**, *clearly rattled, gets up and moves away from* **JACK** *who follows him. They slowly circle the room.* **JACK***'s back is visibly bothering him.*)

JACK. Oh yeah?

WASHINGTON. Yes, it was me. That's right. Me.

JACK. You know, when your voice shakes like this you sound just like a little bitch.

WASHINGTON. Took the shears from over there and thought I'd do some pruning myself.

JACK. It was a crimper, you pin head. They found it.

WASHINGTON. The last few hits, sure. To tell you the truth, I wouldn't know what a crimper was if I was getting hammered over the head with it. Fuck, I don't even know what crimping is.

JACK. It joins metal.

WASHINGTON. Well look at you Wikipedia!

JACK. You're a cocky son of a bitch. For no good reason. You got nothing. A loser with no future.

WASHINGTON. ...but if that's what I finished her off with, then I'll take your word for it! It was the closest thing of Todd's that I could find that looked plausible.

JACK. Yeah, you wish.

WASHINGTON. The handles are almost identical. *(Laughs)* Come to think of it, I think they might have even been the same brand.

JACK. You're a nut.

WASHINGTON. There she was in her little apron. The look on her face. The look of surprise. Not fear, she didn't it see it coming. She didn't know what I was going to do. I mean, why would she?

JACK. I won't tell you again, have some respect.

WASHINGTON. She called out my name...got it wrong, of course. I don't know why that's so difficult for people to get right.

JACK. It's a dumb name.

WASHINGTON. …but she could never wrap her stupid little head around it. But whatever, I'll say this, at one point I wondered if she had metal plates. Still, got there in the end. Caved in like an old cantaloupe!

(JACK *makes a grab for* WASHINGTON, *narrowly missing.* JACK *yelps in pain and falls to the floor.*)

WASHINGTON. Your back bothering you, Jack? It hurts, right? No golf for you! Rest up! Doctor's orders!

JACK. By God, you're a sick little fuck. With a vivid imagination. Your head's messed up from all that garbage you spent hours watching at the video store. Your poor mother…it's no wonder…she probably took one look at you wrapped in a blanket and ordered you to be sent straight to the shredder! That's the thing with your crop…your generation…you're all vile. You're lazy, you don't get what you feel you're entitled, and you go ruin things for everyone else…it's all drugs, video games and violence with you people… stealing and robbing, internet pornography…walking into schools blowing other kids' heads off…it's nothing but bile. And you piss on the land that gives you all the opportunity in the world. And God knows what kind of music you listen to.

WASHINGTON. You don't give a fuck about her. She hates you. She hates him.

JACK. You're warped. A looney tune with a schoolboy crush on a happily married woman!

WASHINGTON. *Happy?* This is a prison for her. You make it a prison.

JACK. You'll never get to live in a house like this again. A place like this? It's out of your reach and you know it even at your age. That's it, isn't it? That's what hurts!

WASHINGTON. That's why she drinks all the time. And you don't see it. You don't care.

(WASHINGTON *goes and takes the large pair of pruning shears that hang on the wall by the front door.*)

JACK. What are you doing? Put those down, you wacko. Look, you got it wrong. I just wanted the best for my baby. Sure, I've always encouraged her relationship with Daniel. He was always going to do well for himself. He just had that get up and go. But you make it sound like this was some arranged marriage or something. Like they do in those bat shit crazy countries with those nut house religions they have. Will you put those down? Nobody forced anybody to do anything, she's well looked after and as her Daddy I can sleep at night because of it. I just wish you had a daughter, so you can see where I'm coming from.

(*WASHINGTON looks at* JACK *and moves slowly towards him, opening and closing the large pair of pruning shears.*)

Will you please put those down? Sure, I'm sure she and he have their differences from time to time, but that's the same for everybody. That's marriage. Heck, that's life! She's no spring chicken anymore, she dropped out of college, she can't have kids...

(*WASHINGTON is stood over* JACK, *still opening and closing the large pair of pruning shears.*)

WASHINGTON. She can. There's nothing wrong with her.

JACK. ...like I say, she can't have children, I just don't see a whole lot of other options for her at this stage-

(*WASHINGTON raises the pruning shears above his head and as they slam down on* JACK *there is a blackout.*)

Scene Six

(Later. **MR. BEAUMONT** *enters through the front door. He sees* **JACK** *immediately and bends down to see if he is still breathing. He is clearly horrified at the bloody site.)*

MR. BEAUMONT. What the fuck…

*(***WASHINGTON*** *enters from the door leading to the rest of the house. He is still holding the large pair of bloody pruning shears.* **MR. BEAUMONT** *looks up at* **WASHINGTON,** *with an understandable sense of trepidation and confusion. Silence, then finally.)*

Hey, Wash.

WASHINGTON. Hey.

MR. BEAUMONT. How's it going, buddy?… What…what happened?

WASHINGTON. I killed Jack.

MR. BEAUMONT. Okay…okay…sure…why, why'd you do that, Wash?

WASHINGTON. Because I guess I didn't like him.

MR. BEAUMONT. Sure. Yeah *(A beat)* But did you have to do it *today*? I mean…like…everyone's got a lot of shit going on…we could have talked about this, you and me…

(No response)

You…y' know…

WASHINGTON. Yes?

MR. BEAUMONT. You…y' know, Wash. You just can't go killing people you don't like. We don't really do that. There are laws and stuff.

WASHINGTON. You wanted to kill Mrs. Beaumont. I wanted to kill Jack.

MR. BEAUMONT. No, no...no, no... I *did* want to kill Mrs. Beaumont. I *did*...but there was a reason for that. It wasn't because...

(Pause)

(Light bulb) Hey, wait a minute.

WASHINGTON. What?

MR. BEAUMONT. Wait one sec.

WASHINGTON. What?

MR. BEAUMONT. Amber...did what happen to Amber *inspire* you to do this to Jack?

WASHINGTON. *(Sighs)* Jesus.

MRS. BEAUMONT. What?

(Pause)

MR. BEAUMONT. That was *you?*

*(*WASHINGTON *nods)*

No, no way...you fucking...we were going to have a baby ...

*(*MR. BEAUMONT *advances towards* WASHINGTON *who threateningly holds out the pruning shears directly pointing at* MR. BEAUMONT. MR. BEAUMONT *retreats.* MRS. BEAUMONT *enters from the front door. She sees* JACK *immediately and gasps.)*

MRS. BEAUMONT. Daddy? What happened?

MR. BEAUMONT. He's dead.

MRS. BEAUMONT. He's dead? Why...what happened?

WASHINGTON. I killed your father, Mrs. Beaumont.

MRS. BEAUMONT. Why?...how?

MR. BEAUMONT. With the shears.

WASHINGTON. That's right.

MRS. BEAUMONT. My pruning shears?

WASHINGTON. Yes.

(Silence)

MRS. BEAUMONT. And...and are they bent now?

(**WASHINGTON** *opens and closes the large pair of pruning shears a couple of times.*)

WASHINGTON. No, I think they're fine.

MR. BEAUMONT. He killed Amber too.

MRS. BEAUMONT. *Did you?*

WASHINGTON. Yes.

MRS. BEAUMONT. I have to say, Washington, this is a side of you that I haven't seen before.

MR. BEAUMONT. Why do this? Why?

MRS. BEAUMONT. And Amber as well?

WASHINGTON. Because Mr. Beaumont was having an affair with her. Because I didn't think she was a good friend to you even though she posed as one…and I had a couple of issues with her myself.

(**MRS. BEAUMONT** *looks over at* **MR. BEAUMONT** *and back to* **WASHINGTON**.)

I killed Jack because I just didn't think he was a positive influence in your life.

MRS. BEAUMONT. Oh. *(A beat)* Right.

(Pause)

Amber was pregnant.

MR. BEAUMONT. Yeah. Seven weeks.

WASHINGTON. I have to say I did not know this at the time. Whether knowing that would have changed things, I cannot honestly say. *(A beat)* I doubt it.

MR. BEAUMONT. *(Broken)* I was going to have a son. I know it. It may be my only chance.

WASHINGTON. Mr. Beaumont, there is nothing wrong with Mrs. Beaumont's reproductive organs as far as she can tell. She has been lying to you for years.

(**MR. BEAUMONT** *looks at* **MRS. BEAUMONT**.)

Mrs. Beaumont it was only suggested by Mr. Beaumont that I live here because he expressed a desire to kill you and he thought that I could of been of some help.

MR. BEAUMONT. You...you're a fucking little-

WASHINGTON. LET ME FINISH!!!!!!!!!!!!

(MR. BEAUMONT retreats.)

You both may look at me in your lives right now with, I don't know, some suspicion...and Mr. Beaumont, with no doubt, some regret, but by no means...to my coming here, could anyone describe your marriage as healthy. I'm doing all this for you, Mrs. Beaumont. In you, I saw a beautiful flower surrounded by nothing but disease. As a keen pruner yourself, I'm sure you know what I'm talking about.

(MRS. BEAUMONT slowly nods.)

Mrs. Beaumont, you're the most beautiful woman I've ever seen. Ever since you first came into the video store, I've been obsessed with you. You would come in regularly, and for the twenty-four hours or so after those times you came in, I was unable to either sleep or eat.

MRS. BEAUMONT. Really?

WASHINGTON. I took more shifts, came in to help when I didn't have a shift, and sometimes I would just go there to hang out because I didn't ever want to miss you.

MRS. BEAUMONT. Well, that's really-

WASHINGTON. Please. *(A beat)* I always had access to your address but it was only when you started to come into the store less and less that I decided to come here. It was just making me crazy. My mind was racing. "Have they switched to an online service?", "Are they just happier with their cable movie package?", "Do they now only watch on Blu-ray? Or have they just made a conscious effort to read more?" All these questions I asked myself, and it was killing me. Fortunately, you did have some movies out that were due back and so I came over here. When you both invited me to live here, I could not believe my luck. This house, you, it's really all I've ever wanted. I love you, Mrs. Beaumont. You may not be quite right in the head and maybe neither am I. Maybe Mr. Beaumont isn't either. But at least you and I have a soul.

(Silence)

MRS. BEAUMONT. What do you want?

WASHINGTON. I want you, Mrs. Beaumont. I want a life here with you. We can take it slow at first. I'll even stay in the guest house until things between us develop.

MR. BEAUMONT. What about me?

WASHINGTON. I'll kill you.

MR. BEAUMONT. And you'll go to prison.

WASHINGTON. Not necessarily. I could kill you right now and then frame the whole thing to look like you and Jack had an argument, you killed Jack and then immediately felt bad about it so attacked yourself with the pruning shears in an act of remorse.

MRS. BEAUMONT. Can we do that?

MR. BEAUMONT. He doesn't even have a job.

MRS. BEAUMONT. That's true. You don't, Washington.

WASHINGTON. I could probably just go back to the video store. They love me there.

MR. BEAUMONT. You stole from them.

WASHINGTON. I did not *steal* from them. I rented out some movies they had anyway, didn't enter the rental into the computer and I kept the money for myself.

MR. BEAUMONT. It's still unethical.

WASHINGTON. The only person I've ever told is you.

MR. BEAUMONT. Well, I'll tell them! How's that?

WASHINGTON. But you'll be dead *(A beat)* I am not going to spend my life in prison. Mrs. Beaumont...if you won't have me, I would rather just kill myself. There would be nothing else for me to live for. Not now.

MR. BEAUMONT. *(To* **MRS. BEAUMONT***)* Wow, what an offer. You can't be seriously considering this? What are you gonna do? Get a full time job yourself? *(Laughs)* Live off his six bucks an hour?

WASHINGTON. Eight. And like we've said, I have ways of making more. Besides, Jack's dead now. She'll get all kinds of things off that, surely. His house. His savings.

MRS. BEAUMONT. You've worked all this out, haven't you?

(WASHINGTON shrugs)

MR. BEAUMONT. *(To MRS. BEAUMONT)* Honey, life is... complicated and fast. Especially these days. There's just so much to consider and sort out on a day to day basis and you don't have any experience of that.

WASHINGTON. She can learn. People do it all the time. She can too.

MR. BEAUMONT. He's not going to be any help. He couldn't find his ass with both hands! He's nineteen. He's a freak. Your life would be a joke. What would everyone around here say?

WASHINGTON. I would be with you every step of the way. We can learn these things together. Sure, I can't buy you everything you want, not at first...

MRS. BEAUMONT. I don't want that.

WASHINGTON. But I'd make you smile more than you do now. I'd make you happy.

MRS. BEAUMONT. I do want that. I do want to be happy.

MR. BEAUMONT. Jesus. Pass me the bucket.

WASHINGTON. Mr. Beaumont's credit cards are being declined anyway. When we bought these suits, we had to use my card.

MRS. BEAUMONT. *(To MR. BEAUMONT)* Is that true?
It's just a mix up...and they are not *being declined.* That was one card! That was the only card in my wallet!

WASHINGTON. He promised me a job and couldn't deliver that because things were getting difficult for him and the business. That's the truth.

MRS. BEAUMONT. Is that right?

MR. BEAUMONT. No! No, don't listen to him! Things have got a little worse, yes. But we'll be fine. I'm in communication. People always need to communicate! Maybe for a short time we need to cut back on a few things, but everyone these days has to. It's just the climate. It'll pass.

MRS. BEAUMONT. What kind of things? Where do we need to cut back?

MR. BEAUMONT. Hell, probably nothing! Like the wacko says, what we get from Jack. Shit, we might even have it better! This is a no brainer.

MRS. BEAUMONT. Washington, you're a sweet, sweet boy.

WASHINGTON. I'm not a boy.

MRS. BEAUMONT. You're a very sensitive young man…

(Silence)

WASHINGTON. Yes?

MRS. BEAUMONT. We should really lock the door.

(**MR. BEAUMONT** *moves quickly towards the front door and locks the front door.*)

MR. BEAUMONT. *(On returning)* Good thinking, honey. Some asshole comes in for a dump and sees Jack lying there. Jesus. Still, it might've put an end to this fucking nonsense a lot sooner.

WASHINGTON. You were saying, Mrs. Beaumont.

MRS. BEAUMONT. I'm sorry, Washington. Daniel's right. This is what I am. *(A beat)* I'm sorry.

(Silence)

MR. BEAUMONT. You made the right choice. We can work things out. We can make it better.

MRS. BEAUMONT. Oh, be quiet. *(To* **WASHINGTON***)* I'm sorry, Washington.

(Pause. **WASHINGTON** *drops the large pair of pruning shears on the floor. Silence)*

MR. BEAUMONT. So how are you going to kill yourself, any ideas?

WASHINGTON. No. I hadn't really-

MR. BEAUMONT. In the garage. My Dad's golf bag. There's a handgun, bullets are there too. You can do it in there.

(WASHINGTON *looks to* MRS. BEAUMONT, *she looks back apologetically.* WASHINGTON *slowly exits the door leading to the rest of the house.* MR. BEAUMONT *and* MRS. BEAUMONT *are left alone.* MRS. BEAUMONT *is unable to look at* MR. BEAUMONT. MR. BEAUMONT *goes over and pours himself a scotch.* WASHINGTON *enters from the door leading to the rest of the house. He is holding a handgun.* MR. BEAUMONT *drops his glass.* MRS. BEAUMONT *screams.*)

MRS. BEAUMONT. (*Blood chilling scream*) WASHI-!!!!!!!!

WASHINGTON. No, it's not loaded. I don't know how you load it.

MR. BEAUMONT. *Jesus H Christ!* The sooner you are gone the better! Come here, I'll show you. So you know for next...wait sorry (*chuckles nervously*)...moron (*He takes the handgun and bullets from* WASHINGTON, *loads the gun and hands it back to* WASHINGTON) There. Good to go.

(WASHINGTON *walks toward the door leading to the rest of the house.*)

Hey, Chief?

(WASHINGTON *stops and turns around.*)

Can you make sure you do it away from the camping equipment? That's cotton canvas waterproof and it's a fucker to get anything out.

WASHINGTON. I'll do my best.

MRS. BEAUMONT. Washy?

WASHINGTON. Yes?

MRS. BEAUMONT. My Mom's old rug, you'll see it, it's an heirloom...kinda. Sentimental value. It would really mean a lot.

WASHINGTON. Sure.

MR. BEAUMONT. Wait! My dad's old golf bag! If you can. *(A beat)* In fact can you just go against the garage door? *(To* **MRS. BEAUMONT***)* I could probably just give it the hose.

*(***WASHINGTON*** exits the door leading to the rest of the house. Silence.* **MR. BEAUMONT** *goes over and looks at the mess around* **JACK.***)*

Someone's going to have to clean this shit up.

(A gunshot is heard. Silence. **MRS. BEAUMONT** *takes a cigarette from* **WASHINGTON***'s pack on the floor. She puts it in her mouth and looks for a lighter.)*

Honey, please don't smoke in here, fuck.

*(***MRS. BEAUMONT*** *puts the cigarette back in the pack. Silence.)*

I need a new glass. Do you want to go see?

MRS. BEAUMONT. No…you look. I can't. And I should say goodbye to Daddy.

MR. BEAUMONT. I'm so sorry, honey. *(A beat)* He was a remarkable man. Top of the line. *(Exhales)* What a week.

*(***MR. BEAUMONT*** *exits the door leading to the rest of the house.* **MRS. BEAUMONT** *walks over to* **JACK***, looks at him and prods him gently with her foot. Another gunshot is heard which makes* **MRS. BEAUMONT** *jump out of her skin.* **WASHINGTON***, carrying the handgun, enters briskly from the door leading to the rest of the house.)*

WASHINGTON. I'm giving you another chance to reconsider.

MRS. BEAUMONT. You! What did you do?!

WASHINGTON. I shot Mr. Beaumont.

MRS. BEAUMONT. Oh! And is he dead now?

WASHINGTON. I shot him in the face.

MRS. BEAUMONT. But you, you look fine!

WASHINGTON. Well, I didn't shoot myself. I just fired the gun.

MRS. BEAUMONT. You are just something else.

WASHINGTON. Well?

MRS. BEAUMONT. Well? Oh well you're putting me on the spot I... I don't know, I... No, Washy. No. It's not you really it's-but- No, I'm sorry...

WASHINGTON. I did all this for you.

MRS. BEAUMONT. I know. I believe you. You're such a martyr.

WASHINGTON. Wait, are you *criticizing* me?

MRS. BEAUMONT. No! Why on earth would you think that?

WASHINGTON. "You're such a martyr".

MRS. BEAUMONT. Is that how it sounded?

WASHINGTON. *(Fighting tears)* Well, kinda.

MRS. BEAUMONT. No, I didn't mean it like that at all! You are, baby. You're such a martyr.

WASHINGTON. There! You did it again!

MRS. BEAUMONT. I did not!

WASHINGTON. Oh listen, just forget it!

(Silence)

Well are you going to be okay?

MRS. BEAUMONT. I hope so. Yes. Probably.

WASHINGTON. I mean, I can take you with me?

MRS. BEAUMONT. Where?

WASHINGTON. Wherever we go next. You said-

MRS. BEAUMONT. *(Appalled)* Oh God, no. No. I don't. Not that. No. I'm sorry. But no.

(Pause)

WASHINGTON. You know, we had something. A connection. Kinda. All those great talks.

(Silence)

WASHINGTON. You're capable of anything. You know that, right? Wherever I go next, I'll be waiting for you.

MRS. BEAUMONT. Oh, Washy.

(Silence)

You are just too much.

(**WASHINGTON** *exits the door leading to the rest of the house. Silence.* **MRS. BEAUMONT** *goes over to the cigarettes and takes one out and puts it her mouth. She finds a lighter. A gunshot is heard. She lights the cigarette and begins to smoke. The phone rings, she doesn't move. Lights fade on* **MRS. BEAUMONT**.*)*

End of Play